"All over this nation, God is stirring the hearts of men to rise up and enter into their God-given destiny. Lou Turner's lifelong passion is to see men enter into their divine purpose in life. 'Living Life God's Way,' of which this book is a part, is born out of this passion. Throughout this Bible study series, Turner opens up God's Word to help you discover HIS plan for your success in your life, family, and work. If you are ready to get off the treadmill, to begin to enjoy God's fullness in your life and make a significant contribution to the world around you, I recommend that you dive into this life-transforming Bible study."

Hal H. Sacks, D.Min., *BridgeBuilders International Leadership Network*

"It seems North American culture is rapidly moving toward what the Bible calls 'everyone doing what is right in his own mind' (Judges 21:25). The prophet Isaiah declared, 'Woe to those who call evil, good, and good, evil' (Isaiah 5:20). This Bible study series will challenge every man in the 21st century as 'iron sharpens iron'! The Q&As at the end of each chapter really personalize the teaching."

Dennis Conner, *Co-Founder/President, Called to Serve Prayer-Coaching Ministry*

"I have known Lou Turner for over twenty years. Lou loves Jesus and has built his life on the Word of God. Lou's Bible study series, 'Living Life God's Way,' is full of biblical truth that has been tested and can be applied by disciples of Jesus in practical ways. These books will help you grow in your faith and gain confidence and competence, which will increase your fruitfulness in Christ.

Mark Buckley, *Founding Pastor of Living Streams Church*

Living Life God's Way

Understanding Authority

Lou Turner

Understanding Authority
First Edition Trade Book, 2020
Copyright © 2020 by Lou Turner

Understanding Authority is part of the Living Life God's Way Series by Lou Turner.

All rights reserved. No part of this publication may be reproduced, stored in a retrieval system, or transmitted in any form by any means—electronic, mechanical, photocopy, recording, or otherwise—except for brief quotations in critical reviews or articles, without the prior permission of the publisher, except as provided by U.S. copyright law.

Unless otherwise marked, Scriptures are taken from the ESV® Bible (The Holy Bible, English Standard Version®) copyright © 2001 by Crossway Bibles, a publishing ministry of Good News Publishers. ESV Text Edition: 2016. The ESV® text has been reproduced in cooperation with and by permission of Good News Publishers. Unauthorized reproduction of this publication is prohibited. All rights reserved.

Scriptures marked NKJV are from the New King James Version®. Copyright © 1982 by Thomas Nelson. Used by permission. All rights reserved.

Some of the anecdotal illustrations in this book are true to life and are included with the permission of the persons involved. All other illustrations are composites of real situations, and any resemblance to people living or dead is coincidental.

ISBN: 978-1-7331186-1-3

To order additional books:
www.amazon.com
www.hislifeinus.com

Editorial and Book Packaging: Inspira Literary Solutions, Gig Harbor, WA
Book Design: PerfecType, Nashville, TN
Cover Design: MTWdesign, Dickson, TN

Printed in the USA by Ingram Spark

He will be like a tree firmly planted by streams of water,
Which yields its fruit in its season
And its leaf does not wither;
And in whatever he does, he prospers.

Psalm 1:3

TABLE OF CONTENTS

Preface   ix

How to Use This Book   xi

Introduction to Understanding Authority   xiii

1. Resist or Obey?   1

2. At the Heart of Authority   11

3. Serving an Imperfect Authority   19

4. When We're the Authority   29

5. Exercising Spiritual Authority   39

A Final Word   47

About the Author   49

PREFACE

We live in a world that has largely forgotten what manhood is about. In the Western world, men are often portrayed on television as buffoons who are out of touch and must rely on their wives to straighten them out. These characters are portrayed as silly, insensitive, lacking common sense, and when they do speak, they are usually wrong. They are generally portrayed as either ridiculously weak or overly macho. They are not able to commit to a long-term relationship and often mistreat women. Positive role models are hard to find in the media.

However, the Bible teaches a different type of manhood, the authentic one. Men are to be leaders, loving their wives and children, excelling in their work, and standing for truth. They are to be men of wisdom, knowledge, having godly character and seeking after God and His direction. They are to be exhibiting godly leadership at church, in the community, and in business, and to be a light to those around them. They are to be men of compassion and love, as well as courageous and bold when needed.

Men go astray from these ideals, including Christian men, due to improper convictions or beliefs about life. They have received these from various sources: well-meaning family and friends, the media, and the culture around them—a world system that promotes the tearing down of God's biblical truths.

But without proper biblical foundation, we will all go astray.

PREFACE

That's why I wrote these books, containing insights, observations, and biblical truths distilled over the course of my decades of life and ministry. Each section is designed to be a stand-alone section for study and consideration. I hope this series, *Living Life God's Way*, will be used to disciple men in biblical truths for life. Whether you use it for yourself, with a group, or to mentor or disciple someone else, my hope is that it will be a blessing to you and encourage you to seek God and grow in Him.

HOW TO USE THIS BOOK

What does it mean to be a "good" husband and father?
How do I live out the Christian life at work?
What does God want from me—and how am I supposed to find that out?

These were questions that plagued me as a young man—questions, I learned, that are at the front of many men's minds at various times in their lives. For me, these questions began my quest to seek God and discover the answers, and my discoveries, over the years of my life, led to this series of booklets, *Living Life God's Way*. The series discusses 13 topics that every man must deal with, regardless of his work, calling, profession, or circumstances. It is difficult to know how to live the Christian life without understanding what God says about these areas of life.

These topics are:

1. Seeking and Finding God
2. Who You Are in Christ
3. A Man's Work and Ministry
4. A Man and Authority
5. A Man and His Wife
6. A Man and His Children
7. Getting Guidance from God

8. Overcoming Strongholds
9. A Man and Money
10. Repentance, Forgiveness, and Restitution
11. Being a Leader
12. A Man and Sex
13. The Test of Pride

You can use these books to study on your own, in a small group, or with a larger group of men. Each topic or booklet is a stand-alone study, and a person can begin with any one he chooses. They are different lengths and can be adapted to various settings—home, church, or community—all topics that are pertinent to today.

Explore what the Bible says about these important and critical areas. The encouragement is to read these with an open heart, asking God to reveal His truth to you in each of these areas of life. Pray that His Spirit will show you His truth, so that you may live in it and enjoy all God has for you. I pray that you experience the blessing and presence of God in your life as you draw closer to Him and more aware of His leading in every area of your life.

INTRODUCTION TO UNDERSTANDING AUTHORITY

Authority is not a popular topic. We all want to do as we like and dislike being told what to do. Part of this resistance is good, in that we do not want to be led astray or be harmed by others. There is a healthy desire to be independent. But there is also part of us that rebels against authority, even good authority, because we do not want to be told what to do and be under another's authority. This resistance is a part of the fallen sin nature. Some of us resist it more than others, but we all tend to want to be *the* authority—at least in our own lives.

Not understanding certain essential Biblical truths can open the door for adversity to come into our lives. Authority is one of those issues. Failure to understand biblical principles of authority not only can result in hardship or adversity, but in some circumstances can also lead to devastation.

Understanding and practicing biblical principles of authority will bring God's blessing on our lives. There is actually safety and peace associated with practicing these principles.

In this study, we will focus first on positional authority, which is being under the authority of others, and then look at spiritual authority, which is being under God's authority. Join me as we look at these principles—they are keys that can unlock great blessing in your life!

Chapter 1

Resist or Obey?

The young man was of royal descent. However, a foreign king had invaded his land and he now found himself a captive in the court of his conqueror. He had been selected from among many to undergo three years of training by the king's best tutors in the ways of the kingdom. After that time, he would be presented before the king to see if he was found adequate for service. There was opportunity here for a good life, even as a captive.

This king was powerful; his subjects did not disobey him. He was known to demand loyalty and obedience. The sentence for not complying could be death.

Since the young man lived on the palace grounds, he was provided with choice food and wine. But while some would have enthusiastically embraced this benefit, for this particular young man it was a crisis. When he saw the table spread in front of him, he realized his faith would not allow him to eat these foods; they were forbidden. To refuse would jeopardize not only his position but possibly also his life. He wanted to please God and follow His laws, but at what price? He could have reasoned, "Surely God understands I need to eat the food provided for me. After all, God has raised me up to this position and He doesn't want me to blow it. If I do well and gain the king's favor, I will be in a position to help many others, including my family and my people. I mean, we're just talking food here, right? Why should food keep me from my destiny? Let's not get hung up on food; let's look at the bigger picture here. After all, God wants me to succeed."

But Daniel did not take that approach of compromise. After much prayer and consideration, the young man decided to obey God whatever the cost. However, God gave him wisdom. He drafted an appeal that would both serve the interests of the king and keep the young man from violating his conscience.

The young man called the king's representative who had charge over him and made a proposal. He asked if he and his three companions could eat vegetables and drink water instead of the rich food and wine. After ten days, the representative could examine them and determine if they looked healthy and strong, which was the king's ultimate objective. The representative agreed.

At the end of ten days, their countenances looked better and healthier than the other young men in the same program. The young man's superiors gave him favor and allowed him to eat as he desired. At the end of the three years, he and his companions went before the king for the interview and were found wiser and more capable than their peers. They entered the king's service, where they excelled.

This story is about Daniel, a man who had a heart for God (see Daniel 1). Daniel's account illustrates a classic dilemma many of us face: Do we please those in authority over us, or please God?

Resist our authorities or obey them? Daniel made the right choice. He would not compromise his faith and do what God's Word said he shouldn't do. However, instead of a rebellious "No, I won't do that," Daniel asked God for wisdom in how to handle the situation. He came up with an alternative that would serve the best interest of his authority without violating his walk with God, and then made an appeal. Daniel is an excellent example of how a man both follows authority and follows God.

It's true that if all of his appeals had failed, Daniel would have been forced to take a stand that could have cost him his life. However, God's favor on him caused him to succeed and find the favor of those over him.

God's Chain of Command

In life, we will always be under some form of human authority. God uses an authority structure, or chain of command, to bring discipline and order. It is designed for our protection and to bring direction and greater productivity. One of the Bible's plainest commands regarding authority is found in Romans:

> *Let every soul be subject to the governing authorities. For there is no authority except from God, and the authorities that exist are appointed by God. Therefore whoever resists the authority resists the ordinance of God, and those who resist will bring judgment on themselves. (Romans 13:1-2, NKJV)*

The principle of obeying authority is clear from this passage in Romans. Hebrews 13:17 adds,

> *Obey those who rule over you, and be submissive, for they watch out for your souls, as those who must give account. Let them do so with joy and not with grief, for that would be unprofitable for you.*

After the apostle Paul said to "be subject to the governing authorities," he went on to explain how God placed these authorities over us. The reason we obey authority is that we are, ultimately, under God's authority. In submitting to those He has placed over us, we submit to Him. However, failing to obey rightful authority *will* have consequences.

> *For rulers are not a terror to good works, but to evil. Do you want to be unafraid of the authority? Do what is good, and you will have praise from the same. For he is God's minister to you for good. But if you do evil, be afraid; for he does not bear the sword in vain; for he is God's minister, an avenger to execute wrath on him who practices evil. Therefore you must be subject, not only because of wrath but also for conscience' sake. For because of this you also pay taxes, for they are God's ministers attending continually to this very thing. Render therefore to all their due: taxes to whom taxes are due, customs to whom custom, fear to whom fear, honor to whom honor. (Romans 13:3-7)*

But what if the authority is ungodly? What if those in authority over us want us to do something wrong? Let us consider this problem.

Difficult Choices

Remember how Daniel was unwilling to break God's law in order to serve the king? Because he prayed and sought God, God gave him wisdom to come up with an alternative, which the king's representative honored.

Later, Daniel faced another dilemma under the service of a subsequent king (see Daniel 6). The king wanted to favor Daniel highly and decided to set Daniel over the entire kingdom, second only to himself. The other governors and administrators, who were jealous of him and perhaps didn't like Daniel's high standards, couldn't bear to see Daniel being promoted over them, and looked for a way to discredit him. If they were corrupt, Daniel's promotion could have meant their demise. Yet they couldn't find any way to accuse him of wrongdoing.

So, they formed a devious plan and presented it to the king: For thirty days, if anyone were to petition any god except the king, that person would be thrown into a den full of hungry lions. I'm sure this appealed to the king's ego. They knew Daniel prayed three times a day without fail, and they planned to use this to trap him. The king signed the petition, and Daniel was informed of the decree.

Daniel resolved that he would not stop praying, even though his life was at stake. At his regular time, he went home to pray. He knew he was breaking the law, but he also knew that obeying God in this case took precedence over obeying man. He could not obey man if it meant not honoring God and praying to Him. In this case, man's law transgressed God's law, and Daniel knew he must obey God. The men who had schemed against him came into his house, found him praying and asking God for help, and accused him before the king.

In dismay, the king realized he had been tricked. He wanted to save Daniel, but the law had been signed and Daniel had broken it. In that kingdom, once the king signed a decree, it could not be broken. The king felt trapped. There was no alternative. Daniel was thrown to the lions. The end of the story is that God gave the help Daniel was asking for: the lions didn't touch him. As a result, Daniel gained greater respect from the king—and further promotion.

However, what if God had chosen not to deliver Daniel and allowed him to die for his faithfulness? Throughout history as well as today, many have died who were unwilling to deny their faith in God.

The apostles faced a similar choice in the early days of the Church. The religious leaders of Israel commanded Peter and John to stop preaching in the name of Jesus Christ. Peter replied, "Whether it is right in the sight of God to listen to you more than to God, you judge. For we cannot but speak the things which we have seen and heard" (Acts 4:19-20). And they went back to preaching.

Both of these accounts demonstrate that we are to respect and obey authority unless it violates God's Word. Then we are to obey God and leave the results up to Him. He may deliver us or allow us to suffer, but we are to obey God when that choice comes.

Surrender with Wisdom

Thus, both by example and teaching, the Bible is clear that we are to submit to the authority God has placed over us. Doing so honors God. We may not always agree with those in authority. But we are to have a submissive attitude and obey unless they ask us to do something illegal, immoral, unethical, or unscriptural.

Those in authority over us may not be fair or just. But if we are threatened, troubled, defamed, or reviled, we are not to respond in kind. First Peter tells us it is better to suffer for doing good than evil:

> *And who is he who will harm you if you become followers of what is good? But even if you should suffer for righteousness sake, you are blessed. "And do not be afraid of their threats, nor be troubled.". . . For it is better, if it is the will of God, to suffer for doing good than for doing evil. (1 Peter 3:13-14,17)*

Again, not easy! Yet if God has allowed this for us, then He will always be there to help us.

Often we can discern what those in authority desire and come up with a solution that will accomplish their purposes without compromising our biblical duty.

I must admit that over the years, at times I've personally struggled to follow my authorities. I've learned some things the hard way—sometimes more than once. I've wanted to be the one in authority and have others follow *me*. At times my pride, willfulness, and a lack of understanding of God's principles have caused me heartache and grief. Yet, to honor others, we have to swallow our pride and choose surrender. Over time, I've learned to trust God in this area and surrender more to Him. I've asked God to change my heart toward authority and trust Him to work through those in authority over me.

QUESTIONS FOR REFLECTION AND DISCUSSION

1. How would you rate your ability to "be subject" to the authorities over you? Place a mark on the appropriate place on the following scale.

   I do pretty well.   This is a major struggle.

   Please explain your answer—what does this look like in your own life?

   _____
   _____
   _____
   _____

2. Has someone in authority over you ever asked you to do something that would cause you to lie, compromise, or misrepresent something or someone? If so, how did you respond?

3. Consider what you would do if you were to be asked to do something your employer thought was in his best interest and you knew it was wrong. What would you:

   . . . say to God?

   . . . say to your employer?

TAKE A KNEE

Let's kneel and pray. If you are unable to kneel physically, kneel before God in your heart. *"Father, help me to honor authority in my life. But also teach me to honor You in all I do. Show me any improper attitudes I have toward authority. Show me any areas where my heart needs to change. If I have rebellious attitudes, show me and help me to have the proper attitudes that would honor You." (Note: if there are incidents where you have failed in this area in the past and you would like to make it right with God, I encourage you to pause here, confess the circumstances and your own actions to Him, and receive His forgiveness. Remember . . . He is "faithful and just to forgive us our sins and cleanse us from all unrighteousness"—1 John 1:9).*

Chapter 2

AT THE HEART OF THE AUTHORITY

Don't tell *me* what to do!"

Though I didn't say that as a young man, that was certainly my stance toward others. I wanted to be my own boss and make my own decisions. I did not want others telling me what to do. Truthfully, at times I still struggle with it. But I have learned more to honor those in authority.

From walking through life with many men, I know I am not alone in this stance. As men, we can view obedience and surrender as weakness, and resist it with everything in us. When we struggle against authority, it is important to take a look inside and recognize what is motivating our resistance.

Sometimes we want to put ourselves forward and be praised and promoted for our efforts. This is understandable. But we must take caution here. Self-promotion may be motivated by pride and the Bible says that God "resists the proud" (James 4:6). We never want to be motivated by pride. We want our work to speak for itself and believe that God will promote us in His time. We all want others to recognize our work or contribution.

Often, we want to be the one in authority. We want others to admire *us* and follow our opinions, rather than the one in authority. After all, our opinions have value too, and may be better than the one who is in authority.

At times, we might think we have more insight, more understanding, and we see the glaring weaknesses of our authority. We should be the one making the decision. Right?

Wrong.

We may actually have some genuine insight. We might accurately discern weaknesses in our authority. But God is more concerned about our learning to respond properly to authority than whether we are recognized for our wisdom or leadership qualities.

In a sobering Old Testament account, God pointed out two core heart conditions we struggle with regarding authority. Let's take a look at what they are.

Rebellion and Stubbornness

In 1 Samuel, we read of a time when King Saul failed to obey God fully. The prophet Samuel rebuked him, saying, *"For rebellion is as the sin of witchcraft, and stubbornness is as iniquity and idolatry. Because you have rejected the word of the Lord, He also has rejected you from being king"* (1 Samuel 15:23).

In this strong statement, Samuel tells Saul that God compares rebellion and stubbornness to witchcraft. Witchcraft is determining to control our lives through a power other than God. Witches actually seek Satan, or spirits, and their power to lead them. They are deceived into believing that Satan's leadership or guidance is what they truly need and can give them what they want in life.

The key to understanding the root connection between witchcraft and rebellion is found in the Garden of Eden. God placed Adam and Eve in the garden and told them they could eat of any tree except one: the tree of the knowledge of good and evil. It was always God's intention that we learn of evil and its consequences through His instruction and by seeing its consequences in the lives of those who resist following God. He did not intend us to learn through personal experience by participating in evil. God gave us His Word so we could learn of good and evil yet not have to learn everything the hard way.

Genesis 3 tells of the fall of mankind and how Satan deceived Eve into disobeying God. The simple lie he used was to tell Eve that God was keeping good things from her, and that He was intentionally keeping her from experiencing things she would want and would enjoy. He said that if she disobeyed God and ate of the tree, she would actually experience good, not evil. Satan was implying that God was not to be trusted. Eve should do what she wanted and experience what she desired.

That is the root of witchcraft, and the link between it and rebellion. All witchcraft is tied to rebellion and stubbornness against God and His authority. God went right to the heart of the matter, when He said that Saul's rebellion was no different in motivation from those who willfully practiced evil.

Obviously, as Christians we do not practice witchcraft. But we may struggle with wanting to be gods of our own lives and control our own destinies. We all struggle at times with wanting to make all of our own decisions and don't want anyone telling us what to do. When we act in rebellion and stubbornly resist God's authority, our hearts begin to harden against Him.

As Christians, we should want to submit to God from the heart and want to please Him. This is the opposite of rebellion!

Obedience Is a Heart Issue

The book of Colossians tells us that when we obey those in authority over us, we should do so from a heart that fears God.

> *Servants, obey in all things your masters according to the flesh, not with eye service, as men-pleasers, but in sincerity of heart, fearing God. And whatever you do, do it heartily, as to the Lord and not to men, knowing that from the Lord you will receive the reward of the inheritance; for you serve the Lord Christ. But he who does wrong will be repaid for the wrong which he has done, and there is no partiality. (Colossians 3:22-25)*

What a great truth! As believers, we "serve the Lord Christ." Our priority should be to please Him. Therefore, we submit to authority because that pleases Him, not because those in authority are perfect or always right. When we humble ourselves to please Him, God works on our behalf: James 4:10 says, *"Humble yourselves in the sight of the Lord, and He will lift you up."*

If this is an area of struggle, we can ask God to change our hearts so we can obey our authorities with humility and meekness. Asking God to give us humility does not mean we will turn into cowards. Asking God to give us meekness does not mean we cannot also be bold and courageous when appropriate. These qualities are not mutually exclusive. Rather, it is all about the heart. In fact, a heart submitted to God may be led to rise up against evil or wrong for the sake of all involved. Jesus did this. He spoke against evil, against hypocrisy, and against false teachings that were harming people. He showed courage and boldness when it was appropriate.

We need to give our hearts to God, asking Him to change it and make it pleasing to Him. Ask Him to overturn any rebellion and stubbornness and give you humility and meekness, as well as courage and boldness.

When courage and boldness come out of a person who also displays humility, others will take note. They will realize your motive is not pride, but courage and conviction. Our lives are our testimonies. Our actions, attitudes, and work should be an outgrowth of our faith in Christ and our desire to please Him in all we do.

Pray for Those in Authority

Part of our ministry is to pray for those in authority over us. This is especially important if you struggle with the heart attitudes needed to obey authority. The apostle Paul wrote,

> *Therefore I exhort first of all that supplications, prayers, intercessions, and giving of thanks be made for all men, for kings and all who are in authority, that we may lead a quiet and peaceable life in all godliness and reverence. For this is good and acceptable in the sight of God our Savior. (I Timothy 2:1-3)*

Prayer is one of God's pathways to change us. It's hard to have a contentious and rebellious attitude toward the ones we are sincerely praying for. Not only that, the Scripture tells us, we are to pray for those in authority that our lives may be peaceable and it may go well with us.

When we pray for our authorities, God gets involved on our behalf. As we pray for them, He moves upon them for His purposes. He may change their hearts, work through them, remove them, or even move us out from under their authority. But He promises to respond to our prayers. As we pray for God's blessing on them, it causes peace to come on us as we trust God and trust our authority to Him.

We should not take lightly praying for our bosses, pastors, elders, and government leaders. James 5:16 says, "The effective fervent prayer of a righteous man avails much." Never discount the power of prayer! Our prayers both change our attitudes and impact those we pray for, including those in authority.

Surrendered from the Heart

Experiencing God's love and His fellowship means submitting ourselves to Him and wanting to know Him more intimately. If, in our hearts, we want to submit to God's authority and please Him with our lives, we are then able to entrust ourselves to Him as we submit to the earthly authorities He has placed over us.

We have a choice. We can resist God, harbor a contentious and critical nature, and have no peace. Or, we can submit to Him, trust Him, and have peace in our souls. Which do you want? I encourage you to pray and ask God to build in you both boldness and humility, courage and meekness. Jesus had these traits and God desires to reproduce the character and nature of Christ in you!

QUESTIONS FOR REFLECTION AND DISCUSSION

1. We all want our own way. In what circumstances do you especially want to do things your way or be the authority?

   _____

   _____

2. If you have struggled to submit and have a good attitude toward those in authority over you, what makes it difficult for you?

Have you prayed and surrendered this to God and asked Him to give you insight into your situation? If not, I hope you will do so now. Write below any thoughts or action steps that come to your mind.

3. Do you pray for those in authority over you? Do you realize that praying for those in authority over us is both our biblical responsibility and part of our ministry to them and can affect them, our cities, and our nation? How will you respond to this responsibility from now on?

UNDERSTANDING AUTHORITY

4. Do you see humility as weakness? Please explain your answer.

5. How do you think God views humility? Write out your definition of humility below.

TAKE A KNEE

Let's pray: *"Father, help me respond to authority according to Your will—not my own will and stubbornness. Build in me both meekness and humility, as well as courage and boldness. Only You can build a balance of these qualities in a man, and You desire to do so. Help me to respect those in authority over me. Help me also not to compromise Your Word and Your truth, but to live in a manner that will be a witness to others, especially those in authority over me. Make me the man You desire me to be."*

Chapter 3

SERVING AN IMPERFECT AUTHORITY

There was a time when I worked for a hard and demanding man. He was quite successful and wealthy—and proud of his success. I wanted to do well in my work, but this man was difficult to work for. He used a lot of foul language. At times, he did things I considered unethical.

We both had strong personalities and a lot of pride. I was self-righteous, saw the world quite differently than he did, and (of course) at times wanted to change him. As you might guess, conflict arose between us. I wanted to leave his employ but could not find another job. I seemed to be stuck with my job and with him.

One day as I was praying, the Lord convicted me that I needed an attitude change and a heart change. As long as I was under this man's authority, I needed to honor him and endeavor to be the best employee I could. God convicted me that my own pride and self-righteousness were part of the problem.

My attitude toward him needed to be one of a "profitable servant," spoken of in 1 Peter 2:

> *Servants, be submissive to your masters with all fear, not only to the good and gentle, but also to the harsh. For this is commendable, if because of conscience toward God one endures grief, suffering wrongfully. For what credit is it, when you are beaten for your faults, you take it patiently? But when you do good and suffer for it, if you take it patiently, this is commendable before God. For to this you were called, because Christ also suffered for us, leaving us an example, that you should follow His steps: "Who committed no sin, nor was guile found in His mouth," who, when He was reviled, did not revile in return; when He suffered, He did not threaten, but committed Himself to Him who judges righteously.* (1 Peter 2:18-23)

Fortunately, I didn't have to tolerate being beaten physically for my resistance to this man's authority. Nor was he trying to get me to do dishonest or unethical things. Even so, these verses speak to the situation of working for a difficult and imperfect employer. Whether the authority over us is kind or harsh, we are to have a submissive heart toward them. Even if we suffer for doing good, we are to be patient, for this is commendable before God.

This response can be difficult. As a man under a "harsh" employer, I needed to follow Christ's example, be subject to my authority, and entrust myself to the God who "judges justly." While I could not do anything at work that would violate God's Word, I *could* work hard, have a good and loyal attitude toward my boss, and be the best employee I could.

Within thirty days of my attitude change, the relationship changed.

My employer saw the difference in me and realized I wanted to please him and do the best job I could. In turn, his attitude toward me altered. Over time, his confidence in me grew; we even became close. Though we had different values in many areas, he accepted my convictions as he saw them played out in a respectful manner toward him. As I tried to honor him, he honored me.

I realized God had placed me in that position to change me into a man who would honor Him in a difficult circumstance. The change started when I adopted attitudes that not only honored my authority, but God. On a positive note, I learned much from this man that has helped me over the years.

Proverbs 27:17 says that *"as iron sharpens iron, so a man sharpens the countenance of his friend."* As I discovered, the hardship of submitting to an imperfect authority is often an "iron" that shapes and sharpens us for what God has ahead. By the way, everyone is imperfect, including you and me. So, naturally all of those in authority are imperfect too!

Shaped in the Hard Place

God sees the big picture. In my case, rebellion would have kept me from learning some valuable skills for His future purpose for me. God had chosen me to follow Him, and that meant He would also work in me, according to Romans 8:29, *"For whom He foreknew, He also predestined to be conformed to the image of His Son."* God uses our authorities (often, in our workplaces) to change us and develop godly character. He certainly did for me.*

We have already seen how God gave Daniel wisdom and perseverance as he served a very difficult authority. Nebuchadnezzar,

---

* To learn about how God works in us through our jobs, I encourage you to do the study *A Man's Work and Ministry*, in this series.

the king of the ancient empire of Babylon, was an ungodly king who served pagan gods made of wood, stone, and metal. He was given to fits of rage and demanded complete loyalty from everyone around him. He had no problem with executing those who opposed him.

I'm sure Daniel would have preferred a different job and employer. Even so, God had plans for Daniel. As Daniel sought God, he was blessed where he was. He "bloomed where he was planted." God went on to use Daniel under three successive kings, all pagan worshippers.

We would all like to work for a Christian who is kind, gives us lots of praise, is generous with us, and is understanding and patient. Guess what? It usually just doesn't work that way! Most employers or authorities are not Christians and often do not have these qualities. Nebuchadnezzar certainly didn't. He was proud, ruthless, demanding, and at times cruel. But that was where God put Daniel.

In the early years of King David's life (1 Samuel 16-18), we see another biblical example of how a man was shaped and sharpened by being under a difficult authority. David was a young man—possibly in his late teens or early twenties—when God selected him to be king over Israel. The prophet Samuel came to David's house and anointed him in front of his parents and brothers. King Saul held the throne at the time, even though the Lord had rejected Saul because of disobedience, and had declared that his reign would not endure.

What a setting! David knew that God had rejected Saul because of his shortcomings. Most men would probably have looked for an opportunity to take the throne God had promised, by force if necessary. Yet David did not force the issue, even though some might say he had every right to do so. He simply went about his life in obedience to his father as he had always done—tending the flocks of sheep in the mountain pastures, and delivering food to the troops where his brothers served in Saul's army.

God often puts a vision in our hearts that is from Him. The timing and method of fulfillment is up to him. For David, he had to wait for a number of years to see him becoming king fulfilled. This is often true for all of us. Waiting on God and being faithful to him during the wait can try us. But often God is working in us to ready us for what He has for us.

While serving his earthly father, he was given an errand to take food to his brothers. It was on this errand that David killed the giant Goliath and won a great victory for Israel (1 Samuel 17). Following this victory, King Saul took David into his service and put part of the army under his command. David's victories piled up, and all Israel sang his praises. Even Saul came to realize that David would be king. Then, Saul became jealous. He tried to kill David and drove him from his presence. Thereafter, Saul continually hunted David to kill him.

God brought a small army of men to David for him to lead (1 Samuel 22:1-2). Twice, David had the opportunity to kill Saul and take the throne God had promised him. His men even encouraged him to do so (1 Samuel 24, 26). On one of those occasions, Saul entered a cave alone in order to relieve himself, a cave where David and his men were hiding. Saul was in a very compromising position, and David could have easily killed him. Shouldn't he have? Not only had God promised David the throne, but Saul had accused David unjustly and was hunting him down to kill him. It would seem that God had delivered Saul into David's hand. The kingdom God had promised him was in his grasp. His men were telling him to take advantage of this situation and that God had indeed delivered Saul to David.

However, David did a surprising thing: He refused to harm Saul. He said, *"The Lord forbid that I should do this thing to my master, the Lord's anointed, to stretch out my hand against him, seeing he is the anointed of the Lord"* (1 Samuel 24:6).

David understood a profound and basic truth. God had established Saul as the authority. David would be sinning and not trusting God if he took matters into his own hand. David determined to allow God to raise him up as king, in God's time. Because he believed God would deal with Saul when He was ready, he would not take matters into his own hand to raise himself up. He would wait on God.

What a great lesson. When we wait on God to raise us up, He blesses us. David was not only applying God's principles of respecting authority and trusting God, but he was also teaching them to his men. Later, when it was God's timing, God caused Saul to be slain in battle, and David was crowned king. As he endured under a deeply flawed authority, David exhibited great insight about authority and God's ways. God developed great character in David during this time.

Hardship and Blessing

Those in authority over us are not perfect; that's a guarantee. But they *are* in authority. In fact, if you are looking for the perfect boss or spiritual authority—give up; they don't exist!

Our authorities will be wrong at times. This is where wisdom comes in. Of course it's right to speak up when we believe it is in the best interest of our authorities to do so. But the manner in which we disagree should demonstrate that their welfare is our greatest concern. Most employers will value those qualities and come to recognize the good in such a "profitable servant." Even if they do not, they are still in God's chain of command over us. Disagreeing with the boss is not a time for rebellion or stirring up contention. At times, being a profitable servant may mean we need to disagree with our authority for their good, and for the organization's good. We are trying to protect them from making a poor or harmful decision. But in the end, it is their decision.

This does not mean we are weak-willed, or that we compromise our values or do things that are inappropriate. There are times we must remove ourself from an unhealthy circumstance. Someone being subjected to sexual advances at work might need to get another job. And there may be other circumstances that make it clear we need to change our employment. If you feel you are in a position where you need to make a change and believe that is God's will for you, then you should prayerfully pursue that.

Often when we disagree, however, right and wrong is not the issue. Many times, we just want our own way. Is our desire just to please ourselves, or is it to be a godly influence in our surroundings? It is hard to be a godly influence when we are rebellious and stubborn. If we have such a nature, we can try to cloak it with some spiritual reason, but a contentious or critical nature is wrong and unscriptural; it is sin. Whether or not our authorities recognize it as sin, they will not appreciate it.

As a young man working for a difficult boss, God wanted me not only to submit to him, but also to honor and have a servant's heart toward him. As I learned to honor my authority, I really was blessed.

This is a true biblical principle. Responding to authority with the heart of Christ brings God's favor and, usually, favor with our authority. This does not mean we are weak or weak-willed, or that we compromise our values or do things that are inappropriate. Being a profitable servant means our labor, attitudes, and presence bring gain to those we serve. We are a positive force for good, bring our employer profit, and protect his/her welfare with our fellow employees. We do not enter into gossip or allow a critical spirit in our hearts. We should always desire not to sin with our mouth or attitudes.

When God is ready, He will give us the new job, promote us, or change the heart of our authority. We are to trust God and humble ourselves before Him.

Do you think God can work through imperfect people in authority over us? David believed this and God honored it. Realize that God is ultimately in control: *"The king's heart is in the hand of the Lord like channels of water; he turns it wherever he wants"* (Proverbs 21:1).

QUESTIONS FOR REFLECTION AND DISCUSSION

1. In what way have you seen God work through authority to shape you?

2. It can be difficult to trust God to work through others, especially when we don't agree with them or what they are doing. Are you willing to be loyal and have a servant's heart? Please explain your answer—positive or negative.

3. How would you rate your ability to trust God with your future while you endure a difficult present?

   _____
   _____
   _____
   _____

4. How would you rate your belief that when we honor God, He will withhold no good thing from us (Psalm 84:11)?

   _____
   _____
   _____
   _____

5. If you rated yourself low in these abilities and beliefs, what would help to strengthen you here?

   _____
   _____
   _____
   _____

TAKE A KNEE

Let's pray: *"Father, work in me so that I have a servant's heart and am a profitable servant to the authorities You have placed me under. Jesus had these qualities, and I want them in me. I confess that a servant is not a weak man, but a man with strong resolve wanting to honor You in his life. Help me to be like Christ in these areas. Help me to trust in Your timing as I wait for You to raise me up, to give me Your promises. Teach me Your ways. I choose to trust You."*

Chapter 4

When We're in a Position of Authority

What does the Bible teach concerning those in positions of authority over others? If we are in authority, we need to view it as a position of trust from God. In that position, we have the unique ability to influence others for good or evil. Obviously, the Lord wants us to use that influence for good. As we move through life, many of us will be in positions of authority in the workplace and in the church. And those of us who are fathers will be charged with the important responsibility of training our children to honor and respect authority.

In the Workplace

As employers or managers, our actions, attitudes, the standards we set, and our personal work ethic will have a great influence on the culture we establish with those working for us. We are never to use our positions and influence to take advantage of or abuse others. Treating others fairly, having a positive attitude, and acting with honesty, integrity, and truthfulness will greatly impact those under our leadership.

If we are in management in a company, we must not allow those under us to have poor attitudes toward the company or those in authority. We should encourage them to give their best efforts and have good attitudes—and then reward those who do. Our work is not just about making money. It is about relationships, the quality of the product or service we offer, and our influence on others. Our work and our leadership are a large and important part of our ministry to others.

We also want to be sure we pay others what they are due:

> *For the scripture says, "You shall not muzzle an ox while it treads out the grain,' and, 'The laborer is worthy of his wages." (1 Timothy 5:18)*

> *Do not withhold from those to whom it is due, when it is in the power of your hand to do so. Do not say to your neighbor, "Go, and come back, and tomorrow I will give it," when you have it with you. (Proverbs 3:27-28)*

Being fair in financial matters is not only a matter of integrity; it is also part of our ministry. This does not mean we should be careless with money, but just. We should want to reward those who are profitable to us in our work.*

The bottom line: never minimize the influence you may have over others, both positively and negatively. Realize that God will one day reward you or hold you responsible for how you used that influence.

---

* The study in this series, *Being a Leader,* deals with the topic of leading others in more depth.

Authority in the Local Church

There are other positions of authority besides in the workplace. One place is the church. Many men have positions of leadership and authority in their local churches, even when they are not on church staff.

In the local church, those in leadership positions have great influence over others. Different churches have different authority structures. Most churches have a senior pastor and a leadership board. This board may consist of elders, deacons, trustees, or board members. Typically, the senior pastor will report to the board and obtain their input and support for the direction of the church. Beyond that, church staff or volunteers may lead various ministries. Each of these leadership positions is a ministry to others.

The Bible teaches us that in the church, leaders are to see themselves as both serving and leading. They serve the needs of the local church body as they give direction in their various positions. We see this in 1 Peter 5:2-5 where the apostle Peter speaks to elders (leaders) in the church:

> *Shepherd the flock of God which is among you, serving as overseers, not by constraint but willingly, not for dishonest gain but eagerly; nor as being lords over those entrusted to you, but being examples to the flock; and when the Chief Shepherd appears, you will receive the crown of glory that does not fade away. Likewise you younger people, submit yourselves to your elders. Yes, all of you be submissive to one another, and be clothed with humility, for 'God resists the proud, but gives grace to the humble.*

This passage establishes two important principles for church leadership. First, church leaders are to serve willingly, not just for money. This does not mean they should not be paid fairly for their work, but rather, they are serving because they want to and believe God is calling them to this ministry. Church leaders are not to "lord it over" those they lead, but rather perform their ministry out of love, dedication, and obedience to the Lord. They are willing to serve the congregation and see it as their ministry to them.

Second, those in the church should respect and follow the leadership of the elders or leaders. We often view employers as having greater authority over us than other leaders because our bosses hold financial leverage over us and can fire us if they are dissatisfied. However, for the Christian, the same loyalty and respect should be given to all positions of authority, including our church leaders. Unity in the church comes through love, respect, and order.

Obviously, each believer has the responsibility to study the Bible and not follow bad leadership or false teaching. We are responsible for what we choose to do and cannot blame a bad leader for the consequences of our actions. But if church leaders are trying to lead us in the way of the Lord, we should give them our respect and submit to their leadership.

Authority in the Home

The ability to lead well and follow well starts (as do most things) at home. Not all men will be leaders in the workplace or church, but most men will be fathers, and thus a leader at home.

Being a husband and a father is, in God's sight, a very important position and one that carries authority and responsibility. Never minimize the importance of your role as a father when it comes to training your children about how to follow authority. Proverbs says, *"Train up a child in the way he should go, and when he is old he will not depart from it"* (22:6). Part of training our children is teaching them respect for authority. If our children do not learn this valuable truth at home, they will probably have a problem with authority in other areas, and it will be a great hindrance to their lives.

Steve is a man I know who loved the Lord and wanted to honor Him. However, his understanding of God's mercy motivated him to overlook behavior problems with his children. In the name of love, he always forgave and was kind, but he failed to balance it with firmness, discipline, teaching, and instruction. As his children grew up, they grew to disrespect him and became very rebellious. His sons began to get into trouble and eventually went to jail for a time. Unfortunately, they had to learn the hard way. Disrespect for earthly authority caused disrespect for God's authority. Steve needed to train his children in both God's love and God's authority.

With that in mind, following are some high points we want to make sure we are establishing in our homes in order to establish a foundational respect for authority in our children:

The Fear and Love of the Lord

In our relationship with God, we need a balance between the love of God and the fear of God. If we never know God's love, we may be fearful, insecure, and lack confidence in our relationship with God and His purpose for us. Not knowing true love is the root of many personality disorders.

When we come to understand God's love for us, we are transformed. We realize the God of the universe truly loves us and cares deeply for us as no one else can. Personally experiencing God's love will change your life. It did mine.

It is also true that if we do not understand the fear of the Lord, we will be disrespectful of God. Fear of the Lord means a deep respect and awe of Him, accompanied by a submissive heart.

Without this respect and submission, we will not understand that there are consequences when we do not live according to God's truth.

The Bible says God will discipline us for not living according to His ways. He does not discipline us because He is an angry God, but because He loves us. Just as parents set boundaries and forbid certain actions because they want their children to be safe and enjoy the best possible life, so our heavenly Father desires only good for us.

Often His discipline will come in the form of allowing the natural consequences we suffer for bad decisions or living outside of His purpose for us. He corrects us to enlighten and teach us so we can be in greater fellowship with Him and be blessed by a deeper relationship with Him. He wants us to learn, grow and be blessed (Hebrews 12:4-11).

The fear of the Lord brings another benefit. Proverbs 1:7 says, *"The fear of the Lord is the beginning of knowledge, but fools despise wisdom and instruction."* All knowledge comes from God. If we do not recognize this, we may be open to deception. Fear of the Lord humbles us and causes us to seek Him—seeking Him is the beginning place to receive true knowledge from God. In this position, we begin to receive all He has for us. We acknowledge Him, humble ourselves before Him, and seek Him and His truth. *This is wisdom!*

Train Up Your Children

Training our children about authority is critical for their well-being. Our children must know both aspects of God's character—that He is a God of love and a God worthy of respect and awe. They need to know that because God loves them, He is committed to teach and train them as they live their lives. If they do not learn respect for authority—the authority of parents, teachers, church leaders, the law, the government, and especially God—they may suffer hardship in their lives.

We should not teach our children about authority in a heavy-handed manner, but by living as examples. Most of the opportunities for training come just as we live life together. All that we do should be done in love. If children view authority as mean, heavy-handed, and unreasonable, they will grow up to be rebellious, skeptical, or even fearful of authority. They will also begin to view God through that lens, and we will have damaged their relationship with God. But if we love our children, discipline them for their own good, and teach them the ways of the Lord, they will accept and respect authority.*

Children need to know you love them, value them, and want to prepare them for life, even in areas that are difficult. If you are a father, do you set aside time to talk to your children about life, and teach them God's Word? It is important that you determine to do this, and follow through with it.

A father should prayerfully ask God to give him wisdom as to how to teach and train his children, and also pray regularly for them. Praying over your children, asking God to teach you how to love them and lead them, is wise and will bring the presence of God into your family life. This is exactly what God desires to do and He will respond to these prayers and give you guidance, wisdom, and insight.

---

* To learn more on how to lead and train your children, see the study in this series entitled *A Man and His Children*.

Living in and under Trusted Authority

When we are in a position of leadership, God's chain of command runs through us. Just as our heart attitudes are vital when we serve the authorities over us, our heart attitudes are vital when we are in a position of authority. We will pass on to others what is in our hearts.

If we are personally struggling with either God's love or God's authority, we need to begin with ourselves. If we do not understand and experience God's love, we may struggle with being harsh, and lack compassion with those in our employ and ministries—and most vitally, with our wives and children.

As we submit to God's authority, and in turn, to the human authorities over us as appropriate, we will experience God's blessing on us. When we are submissive and obedient to God's authority, we are trustworthy to be in authority over others. We will bring the heart, attitudes, and truth of God to those we influence.

QUESTIONS FOR REFLECTION AND DISCUSSION

1. Are you in a position of leadership and authority over others? If so, how would you describe the responsibility that comes with that position?

2. Do you view your position of leadership as from God? Why or why not?

3. How would you like those you lead to describe your influence on them?

4. What is your attitude toward church leadership? Do you try to honor and respect those who lead the church? How do you do this?

5. We teach our children by spending regular time with them, teaching them about life and how they are supposed to live it according to God's Word. When do you do these things and have these conversations with your children?

6. What would you want your children to understand from you about:

    God's love?

_____

_____

    His authority?

_____

_____

TAKE A KNEE

Let's pray: *"Father, help me to use any position of leadership or influence I have in a manner that is pleasing to You. Help me to influence others for good and to encourage them to live their lives in a positive manner that honors You. May I not take for granted any position of influence I have. Give me the wisdom and insight I need to live my life before others in a way that will encourage them and cause them to want to seek You.*

"Change me so I can accurately demonstrate Your love and your authority, so I am a clear channel through which You can demonstrate Your wisdom, Your love, Your care, and Your leadership, direction, and authority to my children, and to those I lead in my job and my church."

Chapter 5

Exercising Spiritual Authority

Spiritual authority can be defined as "exercising the authority God has given us through Christ."

There are two types of spiritual authority. The first is the spiritual authority all believers have, which we acquired when we became Christians. This authority is ours because of the work Christ did through His death, burial, and resurrection. We enter into that victory and obtain the spiritual authority given to us by Christ as believers in Him.

The second type of spiritual authority is given by God as an additional special assignment or calling for certain believers at certain times. In addition to the authority all believers have, this second type of spiritual authority is granted by God to complete a specific assignment.

There have been a number of very good books written about spiritual authority, but in this chapter, I will briefly go through the concept's major truths as I understand them.

First let's deal with the authority that all believers have. (In another book in this series, *Who We Are in Christ*, I cover this topic in greater detail. I discuss our position in Christ and what we inherit by His work when we become Christians.)

All believers become a priest of God when they become a Christian. This is borne out in 1 Peter 2:9-10 where it says, *"But you are a chosen race, a royal priesthood, a holy nation, a people for His own possession, that you may proclaim the excellencies of Him who called you out of darkness into His marvelous light. Once you were not a people, but now you are God's people; once you had not received mercy, but now you have received mercy."*

This is an impactful scripture. It declares that all believers are now a chosen race, a royal priesthood, a holy nation, and a people for God's own possession. We are no longer strangers to God and under judgment. We are now a part of God's family. We belong to Him. Too often we look to those filling the pulpit as the only ones chosen by God. While they have a calling to minister to the church, all believers need to realize they have a calling on their life to serve God—this means they have the authority to carry that out.

It is difficult to come up with words to describe what this means to all of us. As believers, we are washed clean, all of our sins are forgiven, and we are made God's people. We have inherited all Christ obtained and are His representatives on Earth. The above scripture and the following scriptures need to be meditated on so that what that truth means to you individually becomes clear in your heart and mind and you can begin to walk in it. It will revolutionize your life. The Bible says we are joint heirs with Christ. We have obtained all He has obtained as His joint heirs:

"The Spirit Himself bears witness with our spirit that we are children of God, and if children, then heirs, heirs of God and fellow heirs with Christ" (Romans 8:16-17).

We have been called out of darkness (deception, believing lies from the enemy, and a life of being separated from God) into the light, God's truth, and relationship with Him. Furthermore, we are now blessed and stand holy and blameless before Him:

> *Blessed be the God and Father of our Lord Jesus Christ, who has blessed us in Christ with every spiritual blessing in the heavenly places, even as he chose us in Him before the foundation of the world, that we should be holy and blameless before Him. In love he predestined us for adoption to Himself as sons through Jesus Christ, according to the purpose of His will, to the praise of His glorious grace, with which He has blessed us in the Beloved. In Him we have redemption through His blood, the forgiveness of our trespasses, according to the riches of His grace, which He lavished upon us, in all wisdom and insight making known to us to mystery of His will, according to His purpose, which He set forth in Christ, as a plan for the fullness of time, to unite all things in Him, things in heaven and on Earth. (Ephesians 1:3-10)*

God's plan to redeem us and make us His sons was predestined before we were born so that all believers would become joint heirs with Christ. His love reached down to us and drew us to Him. He now wants us to be His representatives to the world and manifest His presence, truth, and the power of the Holy Spirit to those around us. In realizing this truth, we can begin to manifest the spiritual authority He has granted us. We have this spiritual authority whether we use it or not:

> *That the God of our Lord Jesus Christ, the Father of glory, may give you the Spirit of wisdom and of revelation in the*

> *knowledge of Him, having the eyes of your hearts enlightened, that you may know what is the hope to which He has called you, what are the riches of His glorious inheritance in the saints, and what is the immeasurable greatness of His power toward us who believe. (Ephesians 1:17-19)*

Yes, we all need a revelation of what Christ did for us and what we now have in Him. I want to encourage you to think on this scripture and ask God to give you understanding of what this means to you.

We were sealed with the Holy Spirit when we became a Christian. The Holy Spirit is our source of spiritual power in this life. By His presence and His leading, we can do the works of God: "*In Him you also, when you heard the word of truth, the gospel of your salvation, and believed in Him, were sealed with the promised Holy Spirit, who is the guarantee of our inheritance until we acquire possession of it, to the praise of His glory*" (Ephesians 1:13-14).

In Ephesians 2, Paul goes on to say that because of the work of Christ, we have passed from a life estranged from God to being His child because of His love for us. We are now part of His family to do the works He has for us to do:

> *And you were dead in your trespasses and sins in which you once walked, following the course of this world, following the prince of the power of the air, the spirit that is now at work in the sons of disobedience—among whom we all once lived in the passions of our flesh, carrying out the desires of the flesh and the mind, and were by nature children of wrath, like the rest of mankind. But God, being rich in mercy, because of the great love with which He loved us, even when we were dead in our trespasses, made us alive together with Christ—by grace you have been saved—and raised us up with Him and seated us with Him in the heavenly places in Christ Jesus, so*

that in the coming ages He might show the immeasurable riches of His grace in kindness toward us in Christ Jesus. For by grace you have been saved through faith. And this is not your own doing; it is the gift of God, not a result of works, so that no one may boast. For we are His workmanship, created in Christ Jesus for good works, which God prepared beforehand, that we should walk in them. (Ephesians 2:1-10)

I know I have quoted a lot of scriptures here. But this scripture is especially meaningful to every believer and is the basis for the spiritual authority we have in Christ. God has granted us the power to carry out all He desires us to accomplish. We will have obstacles to overcome and times of difficulty. But as we persevere, we will overcome the obstacles and triumph over the times of difficulty. God has promised that and will work on our behalf to bring it to pass. The above scripture states we are to do the "good works" God wants us to do.

THINGS WE HAVE BEEN GIVEN AUTHORITY OVER

Every believer has areas of responsibility and things God will call them to do. As you obey and seek Him, God will grant you the understanding and wisdom you need to accomplish the things He has given you to do. Some areas God has given you power to be victorious over:

1. Your family
2. Your work
3. Your church responsibilities
4. Things God has led you to get involved in
5. The works of God as we go through life

These are things God wants you to be salt and light in. He wants you to have influence and wisdom and to make the decisions to carry out your responsibilities in a manner that honors Him. We don't need to be superstars. We just need to go about our responsibilities in a manner that pleases Him. And as we go through life, we are to do the works God desires us to do.

Too often, we live in fear that others will reject us if we speak the truth to them. But speaking the truth does not mean being overbearing or unwise in our speech. It *does* mean that as opportunities come our way and as we are prompted by God, we speak the truth to others and do the things God prompts us to do. We are granted this authority by God as His people. He wants to work through us and display His power through us. It is who we are called to be: His servants, being salt (preserving the truth) and light, speaking and living the truth to others. Fear can hold us back. But we need to be His ministers as He empowers us.

FULFILLING OUR CALLING

God calls us to do the tasks He wants us to do. For some, that task is to go to a foreign nation and minister to the people there. For others, it is to be His minister in their home nation. You may be called to serve on a school board, get into politics, start a business, or do any number of things. If God calls you to do it, He will anoint you to accomplish it. As we start serving in that area, we will learn and grow and become better at it. God will use us and work through us.

It is true that some believe they are answering a call to minister and it appears to fail. The apostle Paul had to flee cities and go to others because of persecution. Did he fail in his ministry? Not at all. God was working in his life, and new doors opened where his ministry was accepted and successful. Sometimes God uses experiences to teach and train us for His greater work. As we seek Him, we find that what looks like failure is really a doorway to greater success.

So, if God calls you to do something, He will be with you and work through you to see it accomplished. We will have the authority from God to accomplish the task. For some, they will see immediate results. For others, they will go through God's school of preparation where they see some success but ultimately wait on God bring them into the fullness of their calling.

QUESTIONS FOR REFLECTION AND DISCUSSION

1. What has God called you to do?

   _____
   _____
   _____
   _____

2. Are you pursuing His calling?

   _____
   _____
   _____
   _____

3. How is God helping you to accomplish this?

   _____
   _____
   _____
   _____

TAKE A KNEE

Let's pray: *"Lord, lead me into all You are calling me to do. If I am not aware of it now, make me aware of it and show me what You desire for me to do with my life. I know You love me and will always be with me. I know You will anoint me to accomplish all You desire for me to do. Your Word says You have called me for Your purposes and will always be with me. I thank You for Your faithfulness and Your promises."*

A FINAL WORD

What have we learned?
  We are to submit to authority as to the Lord.
  We are to honor and respect authority.
We cannot willfully sin. If our authority asks us to do so, we must respectfully refuse and leave the consequences to the Lord.

If our authority asks us to do something we know we cannot do, we should pray and ask God for favor. In this case, we are to submit to the higher authority, God and His truth, and obey Him. If we can propose an alternative that is good both for our authority and us, we should propose it.

We are to teach and train our children about authority. They are to learn to obey and trust authority in the home. This means we must teach it both with firmness and in love.

If we are in authority over others, we should view that as a position of trust from God. We must lead and use our authority in a manner pleasing to God.

We are to pray for those in authority over us and see that as part of our ministry to them.

Learning God's perspective on authority is vitally important to us. Submitting to God, learning of His love for us, and putting our trust in Him will bring peace and prosperity to our souls.

Being in authority does not mean we have to always be stern and serious. Love has fun, enjoys others, and shows compassion

A FINAL WORD

and concern. It is a hallmark of the Christian life to have joy in our lives.

Who wants to be around a sour puss all the time? No one. We can be serious about life, and yet enjoy our life, our family, our work, and our relationship with God and others. Jesus loved and forgave. He instructed and corrected. He lifted up the discouraged and taught the truth to those who would hear. So can you!

ABOUT THE AUTHOR

Lou Turner wrote *Living Life God's Way* out of his passion for men to discover God, and to get to know Him and what He has for them. This 13-book men's discipleship series is the culmination of Lou's own journey—a life of seeking God, studying His Word, memorizing Scripture and meditating on it, and practical experience with family, community, marketplace work, and Christian ministry. It also comes, by Lou's own admission, from life experiences of both successes and mistakes, as a result of both good and bad decisions.

Lou has headed ministries, written and taught workshops, classes, and seminars, and discipled dozens of men. Now, he has put into print the things he has learned to help other men along their path and journey.

Most of Lou's growing up years were spent in Detroit and its suburbs, where he was raised in a pastor's home. Following his graduation from university with a Bachelor of Science in Business Administration, Lou and his wife planted and pastored a church for three years. After that time, he felt the strong call of God to return to business.

Over the years, Lou has served in numerous senior executive positions with national and international companies in the real estate and oil and gas industries. As of this writing, Lou is still active in business with his own home building company. He has

ABOUT THE AUTHOR

been married to his wife Joan since they were 20. They have three children and 10 grandchildren and make their home in Phoenix, Arizona.

www.ingramcontent.com/pod-product-compliance
Lightning Source LLC
Chambersburg PA
CBHW021123080526
44587CB00010B/620